3

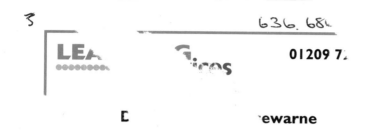

636. 68

01209 7.

LE

ices

C   ewarne

t dat
en

PET OWNER'S GUIDE TO
PARROT TRAINING AND BEHAVIOUR

Annette De Saulles

RINGPRESS

ABOUT THE AUTHOR

Annette De Saulles is a respected freelance writer and editor. She is a former editor of *Parrots* magazine, and has authored and contributed to many books covering all aspects of avian care. Her particular concern is for the conservation of wild parrots and their habitats, as well as their proper care in captivity.

ACKNOWLEDGEMENTS

The publisher would like to acknowledge the help of Christine and Paul Forman (Safehaven Parrot Refuge) for help with the photography.

Photography: Keith Allison and Amanda Bulbeck

Design: Sara Howell

Published by Ringpress Books Limited,
A division of INTERPET LTD
Vincent Lane, Dorking, Surrey RH4 3YX

First published 2002
©2002 Ringpress Books Limited. All rights reserved

ISBN 1 86054 139 9

Printed and bound in Hong Kong through Printworks International Ltd.

Spectacled Amazon Parrot.

CONTENTS

1

Introducing
The Parrot

Parrots and parakeets have been kept as pets for thousands of years. The *psittacine* or 'parrot-like' group of birds comprises of more than 300 species of parrots and parakeets. Their natural habitats are distributed throughout South America, Africa, India, Indonesia and Australia. The lifespan of a parrot can be surprisingly long – up to 100 years for a cockatoo or a large macaw, 50 years for an African Grey, and 25 years for a parakeet.

Among the different parrot species, size and colour differ greatly. The Green-Winged Macaw, for example, may grow to 3 ft (90 cms) in length, while, at the other end of the spectrum, the lively little Budgerigar will reach only 7 inches (18 cms). Colours are found in many combinations – from the African Grey to the Rainbow Lorikeet, the Scarlet Macaw to the Sun Conure – the colourful names speak for themselves.

HABITAT THREAT

Habitat destruction all over the world is currently posing a serious threat to the future of many parrot species. As the rainforest disappears, there are fewer nesting sites and less food. Add to this the horrors of poaching and nest-robbing for the pet trade, and you begin to understand the plight of these birds. If you decide to own a parrot, make sure your purchase does not contribute to this situation (see page 22).

BREEDING PROGRAMMES

Aviculture has an important part to play in protecting some of the more endangered species. Several bird parks and zoos around the world, as well as some dedicated individuals, have combined forces to establish breeding programmes. The aim is to release the captive-bred birds into the wild. Rehabilitation is a painstaking process, however, as the birds have

Opposite: Black-Headed Caique (female).

The Budgerigar is one of the most popular parrots to keep.

to be taught, or need to relearn, how to live in the wild, where to find food and nesting holes, and how to recognise and avoid predators and other dangers.

EDUCATION

As well as attempts to increase the populations of endangered parrot species, there is a need to safeguard and to improve their existing habitat. In some at-risk areas, local inhabitants are becoming involved in educational initiatives aimed at teaching them the value of their country's natural resources, i.e. the indigenous parrots and other wildlife. Eco-tourism, rather than poaching and trapping for the pet market, has been suggested as an alternative means of raising essential finance in these often very poor communities.

PARROT PERSONALITIES

Parrot personalities vary greatly – do not be fooled by the bird's appearance. The Hyacinth Macaw, although the largest parrot and the owner of a very powerful beak, is also one of the gentlest. The Senegal is tiny by comparison, but he has a pushy character and will sometimes try to get his way with a sharp nip. Cuddly, docile-looking cockatoos often turn out to be exceedingly noisy and demanding, while cockatiels belie their diminutive size with their responsive and affectionate nature.

SERIOUS COMMITMENT

If you are thinking of keeping a parrot, take some time to think carefully before committing yourself. Many people buy a parrot on impulse, unaware of the potential pitfalls, such as the noise and mess the bird is likely to make and the amount of attention he will need from his human companion.

That said, a well-cared-for parrot will undoubtedly repay every bit of the love he receives. Most parrots are very affectionate, often comical, and many enjoy learning games and tricks that they can practise with their owners. In addition, some species – notably the African Grey – can produce amazingly accurate mimicry of human speech, singing, whistling and all kinds of everyday household sounds.

Hyacinth Macaw: Large in size, but gentle in temperament.

Green-Winged Macaw: Parrots have very specific needs, and you must be confident that you can provide a suitable home.

THINK FIRST!

Before you buy your parrot, ask yourself, honestly, if you are able to take care of him properly. For example, can you provide him with the right home? You will need to be aware of your parrot's natural habitat. Would he have lived in a South American rainforest, for example, or the hot, dry Australian desert? What would his natural diet have been?

Captive-bred, hand-reared parrots and parakeets will retain their need for the type of temperature, diet, and social interaction they would have experienced in their native surroundings. Parrots are gregarious creatures, travelling in pairs or flocks, searching for food and nesting sites. They are exposed to the elements, and perch on all sizes and shapes of rough-surfaced branches. A natural upbringing teaches young parrots the flying, balancing and manoeuvring skills essential for their survival. Your duty, as a caring parrot owner, is to provide a home that is as sympathetic as possible to these needs.

While it is impossible to replicate all these natural conditions in your own home, there is a lot you can do to provide a stimulating and healthy environment for the species. For example, researching the natural foods of the species and providing him with the right diet will help to keep him healthy. Similarly, providing your parrot with the opportunity to bathe or giving him regular, warm mistings from a sprayer bottle (see page 71) will increase your pet's opportunities for free and natural behaviour.

TRAINING NEEDS

The emphasis in this book is on firm-but-gentle handling and training. These are vitally important, and will ensure that your parrot knows what is expected of him, allowing him to feel relaxed and secure knowing that you are in charge. All parrots will need training if they are to become well-integrated members of the household. Although every bird has his own individual personality, and one should never generalise, certain species exhibit particular traits, or have specific needs, that you should take into account before taking one on. Perhaps the cuddly Moluccan Cockatoo you have fallen for would be too noisy and attention-seeking for you.

Do your research to avoid any nasty surprises later on! Visit parrot shows and talk to breeders of the species that interest you. Read books and magazines. In the next chapter, read about the different characteristics of the most commonly kept pet-parrot species, before making a final decision.

Yellow-Thighed Caique: All parrots need to be trained so that they understand what is acceptable behaviour.

2 Buying A Parrot

Before you decide which species of parrot you want, you need to think about your lifestyle. It is vital to choose a parrot that will fit in with *your* particular circumstances.

If there is no-one at home all day, do not even consider getting a parrot. It is undoubtedly cruel to shut one of these intelligent creatures in a cage, on his own, for long periods. If you are at home for part of the day only, keeping more than one bird may be the best solution, as they will be company for each other. Behavioural problems, such as feather-plucking or screaming, are a frequent result of boredom and loneliness. Remember, you will not have the happy, well-adjusted pet you had hoped for if you cannot give him the attention he needs.

Noise and mess (shed feathers, feather dust, droppings and thrown food) are part of the reality of owning a parrot. If you value a peaceful life, or are particularly house-proud, this may not be the right choice of pet for you.

However, given plenty of attention and freedom, parrots can make wonderful companions in the home. As with most other pets, your parrot's personality and the companionship he offers you will be a result of the care and attention you give to him.

WHICH SPECIES?

If you think your lifestyle is suitable for a parrot, you will then need to choose a species to purchase. The following is a list of the commonly kept, and readily available, species of parrot and parakeet.

LARGE MACAWS

These magnificent South American birds can make affectionate and intelligent pets. However, you should only keep a Macaw if you have room for a really spacious

Opposite: African Grey.

13

The large Macaws will relish the opportunity to fly in an outdoor aviary.

cage, and if you are able to provide a regular supply of natural branches for perching and chewing. A Macaw's powerful beak can be destructive to furniture, curtain rails and skirting boards, etc., so strong parrot toys and wooden items, that can be chewed and destroyed without worry, will need to be provided on a regular basis. Pet Macaws should never be confined to a cage for long periods, and will appreciate the opportunity to fly in an outdoor aviary on fine days.

You will need very distant, or very tolerant, neighbours if you decide to keep a Macaw, as this bird can, at times, be extremely noisy. You should also never underestimate the potential danger posed by a Macaw's beak, which makes him unsuitable as a child's pet.

Macaws will live happily together as friends in a group, although all parrots should be introduced to one another with great care (see page 39). If your pet Macaw is paired with a mate, you will need to be prepared for the fact that he will transfer his affection from you to his new partner.

Finally, before taking on a

Macaw, it is important to consider the fact that, with a possible lifespan of up to 100 years, your pet may outlive you. Before buying, make sure you would be able to ensure your pet's welfare in the event of your death. It is also worth considering that keeping one of these birds has been described as like living with a toddler who never grows up!

BLUE AND GOLD MACAWS
The Blue and Gold Macaw *(Ara ararauna)* is one of the more

The Blue and Gold Macaw is an intelligent and affectionate bird.

commonly kept of the pet-Macaw species. He can grow up to 3 ft (90 cms) in length, so he is not suitable for homes where there is limited space available.

With his good-natured and affectionate personality, the Blue and Gold makes an excellent pet. However, careful training will be needed to avoid aggressive behaviour during the breeding season. The Blue and Gold is a highly intelligent bird who will adapt well to training, enjoying learning tricks from his keeper.

GREEN-WINGED MACAWS
The Green-Winged Macaw *(Ara chloroptera)* is another of the large Macaws suitable as a house pet. He will grow to much the same size as the Blue and Gold. The Green-Winged Macaw is a gentle, friendly bird in nature, but owners should watch out for his beak. The cage must be strong and secure enough to withstand his inquisitive bill.

LESSER SULPHUR-CRESTED COCKATOOS
The Lesser Sulphur-Crested Cockatoo *(Cacatua sulphurea)* is native to the Indonesian islands. The adult Lesser Sulphur grows to approximately 1 ft (30 cms) in

length. Cockatoos are very long-lived, and some individuals have been recorded as still going strong well after celebrating their 100th birthday!

These parrots make very loving and spirited pets, but they demand a high level of attention and interaction, which should be considered before you buy one. If you do not have time for a Cockatoo (or any other pet, for that matter), do not buy one.

Sulphur-Crested Cockatoo: Cockatoos need firm handling, particularly during adolescence.

Cockatoos will usually mimic a few words, but are not renowned for their powers of speech. You can keep your Lesser Sulphur entertained, and out of mischief, with a variety of games, toys and trick training. All these will help to keep this intelligent bird stimulated.

All Cockatoos need to be consistently disciplined to avoid possible aggressive behaviour from the onset of adolescence. Baby Cockatoos are irresistible and will relish lots of cuddles. Remember, though, not to over-indulge your baby, or he will grow into an over-demanding and noisy adult.

AMAZONS

As the name suggests, these birds originate in the northern (Amazon) area of South America. Their friendly, laid-back temperaments make them well worth considering as a pet parrot.

ORANGE-WINGED AMAZONS

The Orange-Winged Amazon *(Amazona amazonica)* is one of the commonly kept pet species, measuring about 1 ft (30 cms) when fully grown, with a lifespan of up to 40 years. Like all parrots, the Orange-Winged Amazon can be noisy at times, although less so

AFRICAN GREYS

The African Grey *(Psittacus erithacus)* is similar in size to the Orange-Winged Amazon. There are two frequently kept African Greys – the Congo and the Timneh. The Congo, with his bright scarlet tail, is more often seen, although the darker-grey Timneh, who has a maroon-coloured tail, makes an equally good pet. For both varieties, the average life expectancy is 50 years. The young of both varieties begin life with dark eyes, which turn yellow as the bird matures.

Greys are undoubtedly the most talented of all parrots when it comes to mimicking human speech. Their accuracy can be uncanny, as well as confusing – as you rush to answer a telephone that isn't ringing, or your dog obeys a command in what sounds exactly like your own voice. Some birds start whistling and saying a few words at just a few months old, but this can vary. However, once your Grey starts talking, you may have trouble stopping him!

African Greys can make excellent pets, particularly when acquired as hand-reared babies, but they require lots of attention and a consistent programme of training.

Orange-Winged Amazon: Amazon parrots are prone to obesity.

than his larger cousins. He will also mimic a variety of sounds, speech and whistles.

Amazons have a tendency to obesity, so your Orange-Winged will need plenty of fruit in his diet, with foods such as sunflower seeds kept to a minimum. His feathers may have a distinctive, slightly musty smell, although the majority of people do not find this offensive.

African Grey: These are the parrot superstars when it comes to talking.

Greys are particularly sensitive, which, in some cases, can trigger destructive behaviour such as feather-plucking (see page 66). Even a new toy, or re-arranging the furniture in a room, can cause stress to these birds, so care needs to be taken when introducing any changes to their routine.

BLUE-HEADED PIONUS
The natural habitat of the Blue-Headed Pionus (*Pionus menstruus*), is Central and South America, as well as some of the Caribbean islands. These birds measure about 11 inches (28 cms) and will live to approximately 25 years of age.

The Blue-Headed Pionus makes an excellent house pet. He is affectionate and attractively coloured, quieter and more relaxed than many other parrot species, and less destructive.

Well cared for, this parrot will make a wonderful, gentle companion, who can be successfully taught to mimic.

Like many other parrots, the Blue-Headed can become obese if careful control is not maintained over his diet. A diet high in fruit and vegetables will guard against this.

BLACK-HEADED CAIQUES

If you want a small, friendly parrot, packed full of character, the Black-Headed Caique *(Pionites melanocephala)* could be just the pet for you. These lively little birds, which come from the northern areas of South America, measure just 9 inches (23 cms) and live for about 45 years. Provided you give your pet the constant attention he craves, you will be amply rewarded with your Caique's affectionate and comical ways.

CONURES

Several of the Conure species make

Black-Headed Caique: Full of fun, but requires lots of attention.

good pets. In their natural habitat, these birds can be found in north-eastern areas of South America. Conures measure about 12 inches (30 cms), and are not so long-lived as some other species of this size – 15-20 years being the average.

SUN CONURES

The Sun Conure *(Aratinga solstitialis)* is one of the most beautiful of parrots, making an extremely colourful addition to any household. Although they are not known for their ability to mimic, they can be noisy birds.

SENEGALS

A popular small parrot is the Senegal *(Poicephalus senegalus)* from Africa. These little characters grow to about 9 inches (23 cms), and live for up to 30 years. Some will develop a limited vocabulary, but they are generally quieter than many other species. Senegals have a reputation for becoming nippy and aggressive as they reach maturity, although this can be lessened with the right training.

LOVEBIRDS

If space or noise are considerations, the Peach-Faced Lovebird *(Agapornis roseicollis)* may be a good choice. These little birds,

Peach-Faced
Lovebird:
Charming
and playful,
Lovebirds
make ideal
pets.

originating from Africa, grow to no more than 6 inches (15 cms), and are less vociferous than many psittacines. They live to about 10 years of age. Hand-reared baby Lovebirds make charming and playful pets, and may even acquire a small vocabulary. However, Lovebirds can be surprisingly aggressive to other small parrots when housed together.

COCKATIELS

An Australian parakeet, ideal for children or the newcomer to bird-keeping, is the Cockatiel *(Nymphicus hollandicus)*. These birds are relatively quiet and are able to adapt to a home where space is limited. Your Cockatiel will grow to about 12 inches (30 cms) and will live for up to 20 years.

There are now many colour varieties of Cockatiel, and these birds are widely available and inexpensive to buy. Choose a hand-reared baby for a friendly, lively pet who can learn a few words, whistles and tricks.

Cockatiels:
There is a
variety of
colours to
choose from.

BUDGERIGARS

Finally, the Budgerigar *(Melopsittacus undulatus)* should not be overlooked. These little Australian parakeets, which grow to an average 7 inches (18 cms) and live for about seven years, make ideal pets for children or for the home where space or funds are limited.

Budgerigars are best kept in groups, two being the minimum you should consider. In the wild, these birds fly in large flocks, so it is unfair to keep them in isolation. Budgies are easy and inexpensive to house and feed, and noise is seldom a problem. These little birds, which respond well to attention and affection, can be easily tamed and taught to say a few words and phrases.

OTHER PARROT VARIETIES

The above is only a small selection of the many psittacines bred in captivity and there are, of course, many other parrots and parakeets from which to choose. Not all are suitable for keeping as pets in the home, however. Rosellas, for example, and many of the Australian grass parakeets, are better suited to aviary life. Lories and Lorikeets, although friendly little birds, squirt their liquid

Goldie's Lorikeet: Attractive to look at, but better suited to aviary life.

droppings over a wide area and are considered too messy for most households! Nanday Conures would be too noisy as house pets for most people. Other species are happier in a pair, or a flock of their own kind in the aviary, and do not take well to domestic life.

BUYING YOUR PARROT

As with any pet, great care should be taken when purchasing your parrot.

Do not be tempted to buy a bird from the first breeder you meet, and be wary of accepting a parrot simply because he is inexpensive.

PRICES

So, before you buy, how much can you expect to pay for a correctly sourced, well-cared-for parrot? The best course to follow is to ask several different breeders what they consider to be a fair price for each of the species that interest you. Use these quotes as a rough guide to the average cost of a tame, hand-reared baby parrot, although do not forget that prices will vary depending on where, and from whom, you purchase your parrot. If you see a parrot advertised in the local paper at a very low price, he is probably an adult bird that is not fully tame, or he may have behavioural problems such as biting or feather-plucking.

WHERE TO BUY

It is very important that you buy your parrot from a reputable source, for two main reasons:
- You should not contribute to the plight of the parrot species in the wild, or encourage the illegal parrot trade, by buying wild-caught parrots.
- You are far more likely to take home a healthy parrot if you buy from a reputable breeder or retailer.

WILD-CAUGHT BIRDS

It is a sad fact that many first-time parrot keepers are unaware that they may be buying a wild-caught bird rather than one that has been captive-bred. Please do not make this mistake, or be tempted by the lower prices asked for wild-caught parrots.

Birds that are caught and exported illegally undergo particularly cruel treatment, often being crammed into tiny containers to avoid detection. A high percentage die, and illegal trading has brought many species to the brink of extinction.

Hawk Head Parrot: It is essential to buy your parrot from a reputable source.

Many wild-caught birds harbour dangerous, stress-induced diseases, which emerge only some weeks after purchase. Expensive vet's bills then follow and it is quite often the case that the bird dies. Furthermore, parrots taken from the wild rarely make good pets. Their natural fear of humans makes them panic and bite when approached and, in many cases, this results in the bird being shut in his cage forever afterwards, his human keeper not wanting to risk another painful nip. This situation is cruel to the bird and unsatisfactory for the keeper, who was hoping for a tame and responsive pet.

Moluccan Cockatoo: A hand-reared parrot will make the best pet.

From this, you will see that it is a false economy to buy a wild-caught bird. It may also support the parrot black market. Only when we stop buying these birds will this cruel trade cease.

AUCTIONS

Bird auctions will often have parrots for sale at low prices. If you are lucky, you may get a genuine bargain at auction, but it is unlikely. There is usually a good reason why a bird is being sold cheaply. Many such birds are psychologically disturbed, suffering from ill health, or stolen. You will probably have no comeback if the bird you buy turns out to have problems, so the best advice is to avoid these auctions altogether.

FINDING A BREEDER

A captive-bred, hand-reared parrot will usually make the best pet. By far the best source for these is a reputable breeder. Avian magazines carry advertisements for breeders in their classified sections. Alternatively, you could contact a local bird club for advice.

Parrots offered for sale by reputable breeders will wear a

closed leg-band, showing that they have been bred in captivity. A genuine seller will be happy to give you a proper receipt, giving full details of the parrot you have bought. He or she will also be able to give you advice on diet and care, and should also offer a back-up service for any queries or problems you may later encounter.

Once you have found a good breeder, be prepared to wait – sometimes for a lengthy period – for a tame, hand-reared baby parrot. Your patience will be well rewarded.

Patience and experience is required if you decide to take on a rescued parrot.

RESCUE PARROTS

There are many parrots in need of a good home, and you may like to consider taking on a rescue parrot. This is not for the novice, however.

Many birds get passed from home to home when they develop antisocial behaviour, and often end up at rescue centres. The reason for the behaviour is usually inappropriate care in the past, which has left the bird unhappy and frustrated.

Bad habits can take a long time to put right, and require a lot of understanding and patience from the new keeper. Nevertheless, if you are prepared for the challenge, your reward will be the affection and trust of a previously frightened or aggressive bird. You may well give a new lease of life to a parrot previously given up as a hopeless case.

WHAT TO LOOK FOR

When you go to buy your parrot, there are a number of checks you should make to ensure that you take home a healthy bird with every chance of adjusting well to life in your home.

WEANING

Your baby parrot should be fully weaned. This means he should be cracking seeds competently and taking solid foods.

ATTITUDE

The bird should view humans as friends. If the parrots you are viewing are kept in flocks, you may find that one of them comes up to the side of the cage to get your attention. Very often it will be obvious whether or not you and a particular bird are going to get on together, and it is a good idea to go with your instincts at this stage.

SEX

Before you buy, make a decision about whether you want a male or female parrot, and make sure that you take home a bird of that sex.

Frequently, a female parrot will favour a male member of the household and vice versa. Many parrot keepers have been disappointed when their pet decides he prefers someone of the opposite sex in the family. Parrots will bond closely, and do not usually change their opinions about people, so keep this in mind.

Some species can be easily identified as to sex. The male Eclectus, for example, is green, while the female is red. Other parrots, such as the African Grey, are impossible to sex without professional testing. An avian veterinary surgeon will be able to undertake surgical sexing, or laboratory DNA-testing can be carried out from a drop of blood or a feather.

HEALTH

If the bird you are buying does not come with a veterinary certificate of health, it is worth arranging one for yourself. Before agreeing to purchase, you should also perform a quick health check, looking for common signs of illness (see page 79).

African Grey: Choose the bird that seems to have a strong affinity with people.

Setting Up Home

3

Now that you have found the perfect parrot and are ready to bring him home, it is time to 'think parrot'. Your home, your family, and your other pets will all seem strange and unfamiliar to your parrot, as will his new cage and his new routine. Try to see the situation through your parrot's eyes. Take things gently and slowly. By gaining the bird's trust with careful handling, as well as establishing consistent ground rules right from the start, your parrot should develop into a confident, friendly bird. A parrot who knows his place within the family 'pecking order' is far less likely to develop behavioural problems later on. Add to this plenty of affection and attention, and you will have a loving and loyal member of the family.

EQUIPMENT
Before bringing home your parrot, you will need the right equipment. Cages and play apparatus are the most important items you will need.

CAGES
Your parrot's cage should be spacious and welcoming, so that your pet is always content to go into it when necessary. A rectangular shape, rather than a tall, narrow cage is best, allowing sufficient space for flying. The cage should also be strong and secure, as psittacines – particularly the large Macaws – are surprisingly adept at undoing catches. Also, a small box, to which the parrot can retire for a bit of peace and quiet when he wants to, may be welcomed.

SIZE MATTERS
You should choose the biggest cage you can afford and can fit in your house. At the very least, the

Opposite: Masked Lovebird.

27

Buy the biggest cage you can afford.

PLACING THE CAGE

Positioning the cage in the right spot is very important. Parrots are highly sociable creatures and will be miserable if they are kept away from the family. The cage should be placed in the centre of the household, in a location where there is plenty of human activity. Sitting rooms are ideal.

The kitchen is not a suitable place for keeping parrots. Birds have highly sensitive respiratory systems, which can be badly affected by the air quality in the average kitchen. One notable danger is non-stick cookware, which, if overheated, can have fatal consequences for your parrot.

Cigarette smoke is another hazard, so make sure that no-one smokes in the room where your bird is kept. Don't use household sprays or carpet fresheners in the room, either, as some products have proved deadly to parrots.

Whichever room you choose, your parrot's cage should be placed out of draughts and away from the television and radiators. Your bird will appreciate a view through the window, but make sure he will not be getting too much direct sunlight. Place the cage against a wall, but ensure that the wallpaper, the window sills and the curtains

cage must be big enough for the bird to fully stretch both wings simultaneously without either wing touching the sides of the cage. Likewise, when your parrot is perching, his head and tail feathers should not touch the top or bottom of the cage. These requirements are absolutely minimal however. Parrots are great climbers – the beak serving as a third 'foot' – so they need plenty of climbing opportunities, too.

are all out of your parrot's reach – or his beak will play havoc with your walls and soft furnishings! At night, the curtains should be drawn, as your parrot may panic if he sees a cat, or any other perceived predator, at the window.

Parrots require a lot of sleep, needing up to 12 hours a night, as well as the opportunity to rest during the day. Bear this in mind if your parrot lives in your lounge. Your bird will be far more responsive to training if he has not been kept awake for half the night with the lights blazing and the television on! In the wild, the sun fades gradually. You can simulate this effect by purchasing dimmer switches, which allow electric lighting to be reduced gradually. These are easy and inexpensive to fit.

CAGE FURNISHINGS
There are a number of cage furnishings which you can buy to transform your parrot's cage into a suitable safe haven and a stimulating play area.

PERCHES
The cage and playstand should be fitted with natural branches of varying thicknesses. Natural perching, such as apple or pear

There should be a variety of perches of different widths within the cage.

branches, are suitable, as are hazel, willow and hawthorn. Carefully wash the branches before placing them in the cage, as disease can be spread from wild birds.

A caged bird will be on his feet all day, so smooth, uniform dowel perches are unsuitable. Some abrasive 'pedicure' perches can result in sore feet. Instead, fit branches of irregular shape and size. These provide healthy exercise for the feet, and will help to prevent the nails and beak from overgrowing.

The African Grey loves to play with toys, but you will need to introduce them gradually.

TOYS

Providing plenty of occupation for a caged parrot is vital for his mental balance. With nothing else to do, this intelligent creature may resort to pulling out his own feathers, chewing his feet or making repetitive, neurotic movements. Like nail-biting in humans, these habits can be very hard to stop once started and are far easier to prevent than to cure.

Purpose-made, interesting parrot toys are ideal for providing mental stimulation when a parrot is confined to his cage. However, the most important factor is companionship – toys are no substitute for this. Buy toys that are strong enough for the species of parrot you are keeping, and vary them from time to time.

African Greys can be frightened by a new toy or perch, so these must be carefully introduced. Leave the new item outside the cage but within sight for a day or two, to allow your bird to get used to it. Let him see you playing with the toy yourself until he loses his fear and becomes interested.

Household items that can safely be chewed and destroyed, such as the cardboard tubes from kitchen towels or toilet rolls, will also be enjoyed. As parrots will test anything and everything with their beak, make sure they are given only non-toxic, safe items. Chains, string and ribbon can get tangled up round feet, wings or beak and should be avoided.

Finally, remember not to fill your bird's cage so full of toys and branches that your parrot has no room to move about!

CAGE CARE

Replace soiled newspaper in the base tray every day and wash perches on a regular basis to avoid the build-up of slippery food waste and droppings. A thorough cleaning of the cage, once a week, will also be needed.

PLAYSTANDS
There are many types of playstand on the market today. You could even make your own. A variety of

The playstand can be fitted with a selection of toys.

natural branches, with a tray beneath that can be lined with newspaper for easy cleaning, works very well. Parrots love to climb and explore, so make the playstand as large and multi-dimensional as possible. Fit food and water dishes on the top perch and add some interesting toys. This will give your parrot a place of his own when he is outside the cage, as well as giving him a change of scene and occupation.

FLYING AREAS
Parrots love to fly, and the need for wing-clipping can be avoided by providing a space for flying that is free of hazards.

If you have the space, an indoor aviary, or even a specially designated birdroom will provide a safe area for free flying (see page 42).

Whenever possible, bring back a bit of the wild into your parrot's life. In his natural habitat, the parrot spends a large part of the day flying about searching for food, so an outdoor flight area, used on warmer days, will be much enjoyed. Here, your bird will be able to experience sunshine and rain – many (though not all) parrots relish bathing in a rain shower – and to move about freely. Logs to climb on or to hide in, safe living plants to nibble at (such as clematis, honeysuckle or pyracantha), rope ladders and swings, will all provide variety and stimulation. Hide seeds and nuts in hanging toys to challenge your parrot's ingenuity.

Some species are hardier than others, so never plunge any bird straight into a cold aviary from the warmth of the sitting room. Instead, acclimatise him gradually once the warm spring weather arrives. Ensure part of the flight is covered over to provide protection against unexpected extremes of weather.

Try to bring a flavour of the wild into your parrot's life.

4 Off To A Good Start

Whard you bring home your new parrot, you will probably be tempted to fuss, cuddle and play with him all day long. However, overindulgence in the early stages of your relationship can prove disastrous.

SOCIALISATION

It is a good idea to start socialising your parrot as soon as possible, getting him used to different people, objects and situations. Remember, though, to supervise him carefully while he is busy exploring. Introduce discipline and simple commands as part of the daily routine, and get your pet used to trying lots of different foods. The good habits he picks up now will become a natural part of his life, and will mean a much easier time for you both later on.

DISCIPLINE

Youngsters will test everything with their beak, including your fingers. Gently dissuade your bird from nipping with a firm "No" and positive eye contact that tells him that you mean what you say. Parrots are surprisingly responsive to human expressions. What has been described by parrot psychologists as 'the evil eye' can work wonders in stopping unwanted behaviour. Avoid shouting and yelling (even if you receive a painful nip). Your parrot will enjoy your reaction and think you are playing a game – biting even harder the next time.

ROUTINES

Accustom your parrot to a regular routine – meal-times, play-times and rest-times. If you are consistent in this, letting your pet know that he can trust you and that you are the boss, he will accept the situation and not scream the house down every time he is put back in his cage.

An ordered routine will help to build up a sense of trust.

Your day might go like this… You let your parrot out in the morning to have breakfast and to play on his stand for a couple of hours while you move around doing the chores. Your pet has had your company and attention during that time, but now you want to do some paperwork in the office upstairs and need to put your pet back in his cage. If your parrot has got used to this routine from the start, he will be perfectly content to amuse himself by playing with his toys, eating, or playing with his toys, eating, or

having a nap until you reappear. He is safe and happy and you can get on with your work undisturbed.

You may discover an alternative scenario if you indulge your bird's every whim, in effect giving him the idea that he is head of the household or 'flock'. Failing to establish a routine or to give your parrot consistent rules for his behaviour, usually results in disaster.

If your parrot is causing disruption in your household, this is probably because he has been allowed to stay out of his cage for long periods, because he always kicked up a fuss when you tried to put him back in and you got fed up with chasing him round the room to catch him. He has not learnt that he must step on to your hand whenever asked (see page 47), so when you grab him, he bites you. You yell and your pet is delighted with the reaction he has caused. When finally back in his cage, he starts screaming for attention the moment you go out of the room. You feel irritated or guilty – or both – so you let him out again. The next day, the same thing happens all over again. Your parrot has got the message that biting and screaming get results, so why should he stop?

The above situation is not only frustrating for the keeper, it is confusing and upsetting to the parrot. However, it can be easily avoided by adhering to a regular routine (see page 33).

BABY PARROTS

Parrots of every age should be subject to the socialisation and routines described above, but baby parrots require extra care. Babies grow up, so beware of the dangers of spoiling that gorgeous little bundle of feathers.

Correct training needs to begin right at the beginning, meaning that you should not rush to attend to your baby bird every time he utters a sound. That said, continual crying by a baby parrot for his keeper (or 'parent'), can be a genuine sign of insecurity. In these cases, the young bird needs reassuring. Get your pet used to being left for short periods. He will know you are around and that he is safe if you frequently talk to him from the next room or as you pass by the cage.

Your baby parrot should be taught that he cannot be with you every minute of the day. It is also worth remembering that baby parrots need plenty of rest, as well as up to 12 hours' sleep at night.

FIRST CONTACT

Your new pet, even if he is a tame, hand-reared baby will, at first, be bewildered by his new situation. He will need loving and sensitive handling.

OVERCOMING FEAR

Some people wear gloves when handling nervous birds, for fear of being bitten. However, these can add to the bird's alarm and, at least with the smaller species, training is better done without them.

A new, nervous bird will need to learn to trust you. If he is really terrified, and flutters wildly as soon as you approach, don't try to force the issue. Parrots have long memories, and how you treat your bird at this stage will have a lasting effect on his future behaviour. Handle him very gently, making no sudden noises or movements, and leave him in his cage to adjust to his new surroundings. Ensure that he is eating during this time by checking for droppings. Try casually putting a small food treat into the cage whenever you pass. In time, your parrot's fear will lessen. He will start to look forward to seeing you, now associating you with something pleasurable (a peanut or a piece of biscuit).

THE FIRST APPROACH

Once your parrot happily accepts your presence and shows no obvious signs of fear, the next step is to accustom him to your hand entering the cage. Take this stage very slowly, using a soft, soothing tone of voice and making no jerky movements as you place your hand inside the cage. As you do so, you might like to offer a favourite food treat. Be patient and let the bird come to you and take the treat. He may allow you

It is natural for a parrot to feel frightened to begin with.

Use food treats to encourage your parrot to come forward and be handled.

to stroke the feathers on the back of his neck or his chest, while he investigates your hand and the enclosed treat. Bear in mind that, if your parrot is fairly hungry when you offer him a tidbit, he will be more likely to take it from you. Plan your feeding and training regimes so that you can use food treats in your taming sessions.

In some cases, it may take several attempts before your parrot has gained enough confidence to approach you. Remain patient, however, and you should eventually achieve success.

DO NOT GRAB

Wrapping the parrot in a towel is a common method of calming a bird too nervous to approach his keeper. However, it is always better to win trust without forceful methods. Remember, also, that picking up a bird by his body, rather than letting him step on to your hand, may lead to a bite because he will feel threatened. In the wild, your parrot would think he was about to be eaten if grabbed in this way.

BODY LANGUAGE

Learn to interpret your parrot's body language before approaching him. If, for example, his eyes start dilating, or he stands tall as you approach, he is scared and may bite if you go to touch him. A nervous parrot may also defecate more frequently than normal. If your parrot is feeling hostile towards you, he may display his aggression by bending low over his perch.

If your parrot puts down his head when you approach, it is a sign that he would quite like a tickle on the back of his neck. However, if he still has his eyes on you as he bends his head, beware – he may give you an unexpected nip.

Other clues to your parrot's mood include:

- Yawning (which simply indicates tiredness)
- Strutting, head-bobbing, wing-trembling and tail-fanning (which are all parts of courtship display)
- Screaming (a sign of frustration, distress, or excitement – although some parrots scream simply because they feel like making a noise).

JOINING THE 'FLOCK'

Once your parrot has become accustomed to you, and to your hand entering the cage, it is time to introduce him to the rest of the family.

YOUR FAMILY

You should train him to sit on your hand and arm, so that he can leave his cage and meet the rest of the family (see page 47). Parrots can become very possessive over their owners. It is a good idea, therefore, to let your parrot spend

Learn how to interpret body language. This Greater Western Vasa is asking for a tickle on the back of his neck.

Children must be taught correct handling. Because of the danger of a bite to the face, encourage perching on a hand or arm rather than on the shoulder.

an equal amount of time with all family members, to prevent overprotective and jealous behaviour later on.

CHILDREN

Introduce children and parrots with great care as each could be a danger to the other. Children should be shown correct and respectful handling techniques and should always be supervised. Budgerigars and small parakeets are a much safer choice of pet for a small child than larger parrots.

OTHER BIRDS

If you already own one bird and you want to introduce another, first have your new parrot checked by an avian vet. You should also quarantine him in a separate part of the house for 30 days.

There is no guarantee that two birds will get along, so always introduce a newcomer with great care. Before letting the birds out together in the same room, leave them in their separate cages where they can see each other, until you are confident they are getting on well. Keep watching for any signs of aggression. For example, even if only one bird is let out and lands on the cage of the other, he may get his toes seriously bitten. Try to

Parrots should be confined to their separate cages for a period so that they can become accustomed to each other before meeting in the open.

A display of aggression will hopefully be short-lived.

prevent your original bird from becoming jealous by giving him as much attention as the newcomer.

Where several birds are kept, there will usually be a flock leader. The other birds will take their lead from him. A pecking order will be established among the birds, with particular friendships and idiosyncrasies developing. The most important thing, though, is that you remain the overall boss.

If you keep several birds and have the space, a separate room dedicated to them means they can be free-flying during the day, with large natural branches, swings and ropes to keep them busy. Giving your pets this extra space and freedom will help to foster good relations between them.

OTHER PETS

In the wild, parrots would be natural prey for dogs and cats. Your new bird may be terrified if approached by your other pets, however innocently, so keep them away from the cage during your parrot's initial acclimatisation period. In many households, animals and birds get along well and are allowed to mix, but this is not recommended without careful supervision.

FREE PERIODS

A parrot unused to being in his cage will be miserable and disruptive when he is eventually confined. Likewise, if never let out, your parrot will want to rush back to the safety of his cage as soon as he finds himself free. Start as you mean to go on, establishing a regular routine of cage-time and free periods.

Your parrot should be given plenty of opportunity to fly around the house, unrestricted by the confines of his cage. However, never leave him unsupervised. There are a number of precautions you can take to minimise the risk of accidents.

A rare friendship: It goes without saying that all interactions between parrots and other pets should be very carefully supervised.

Check for hazards before allowing your parrot free access to a room.

HOUSEHOLD HAZARDS

While your parrot is out of his cage, put a protective guard in front of open fireplaces, and cover open-topped fish tanks. Accidents can happen when a parrot is perched on top of an open door, so make sure other family members are always aware of your bird's whereabouts.

Before allowing your parrot out of his cage, remove everything that could be harmful to him. Pot-pourri, for example, can be poisonous. Finally, for your own sake, put all breakable and valuable objects well out of harm's way before they are knocked off the shelf or shredded!

While your parrot is enjoying his free time, keep a close eye on him. If everything goes quiet, he may be chewing on an electric wire!

FREE FLYING

Many parrot owners are unwilling to clip their parrot's wings (see page 60). However, an out-of-control, free-flying bird will not respond to training and is at risk from hazards within the home, as well as from possible escape. It is vital that, if you do not have your parrot's wings clipped, your bird is well trained to avoid such hazards.

US parrot keeper and writer E.B. Cravens, who promotes close-to-nature bird-keeping methods, teaches his flighted parrots where glass windows and doors are by taking his bird to the glass and gently tapping the beak against it. By doing this a few times, the bird comes to understand where he cannot safely go. You could also attach stickers or mobiles over windows.

If your parrot does escape, training him to come when called may help to reunite you. Teach a specific command or whistle that means your bird must come to you at once. Practise this regularly until it is second nature to your parrot. Even with clipped wings, flight is still possible and, if your pet escapes, he will become disorientated. Your call should prompt him to return to you instinctively.

HARNESSES
Parrot harnesses have now been on the market for a few years. They are proving very successful with many parrot keepers who wish to take their birds out with

them. As any unfamiliar object or experience can cause stress to parrots, introduce the harness gradually, getting your bird used to seeing and playing with it, before you attempt to fit it. Parrots that take to the idea enjoy going out in the car or on visits to friends, and this is fun for the keeper too. However, some birds will be frightened by the feeling of a harness and may never accept wearing one.

Other keepers use leg chains when taking their birds outside, but these are not recommended. Even a tame bird may be suddenly alarmed and try to fly off, the likely result being a broken leg.

Spectacled Amazon: Try teaching your parrot a specific command that means "Come".

5

Socialisation And Training

Parrots live a long time and if training is done with love and patience – just a few minutes every day – it will benefit your whole future relationship.

Training a bird is not about trying to change his natural character, intimidating him or 'humanising' him, but rather about teaching him what is acceptable behaviour. Once your parrot is clear about the boundaries, he will be free to express his own special personality.

Before starting training, the species, size and individual personality of your parrot all need to be taken into consideration. For instance, a young, tame bird will respond and learn far more quickly than an older, previously untrained one. Understand what motivates your bird and work with this. If he gets enjoyment from something, he will want to do it again.

BEHAVIOURAL TRAINING

Early discipline and training are crucial for controlling a pet parrot, particularly once he reaches adolescence and starts to push his weight around. If he has always accepted your authority without question, any behaviour regression during this time can be kept within manageable limits.

An out-of-control bird is at risk from potential dangers around the home. You need to be confident that, if and when necessary, your parrot will fly to your hand or arm on command. A tame and trusting bird, in the event of an accident or illness, will be much easier to catch and examine than one that is afraid of human hands.

CAPTIVE-BRED PARROTS

It is never too early to start training. A baby parrot hearing the words "Up" or "Down", every time he steps on to your hand or is put back on to his

Opposite: Yellow-fronted Amazon.

45

playstand, will quickly learn what is required of him.

WILD-CAUGHT PARROTS

With time and patience, amazing results can be achieved with even the worst behaved of birds. However, a wild-caught adult may never become fully tame or trainable. He may not forget the trauma of capture and imprisonment by humans, who, in the parrot's mind, remain something to be feared. With your patience and compassion, the bird will come to know that he can trust you and will, in time, become a manageable pet, but he may never accept being handled.

UNDERSTANDING 'PECKING ORDER'

In the wild, parrots live in flocks, with the dominant parrot assuming the role of flock leader. In your household, your bird needs to understand that the flock leader is you. Behavioural problems normally stem from the parrot being unsure about his position in the flock, and what is expected of him. Without firm controls, he will try to take on the dominant role, with screaming and biting being the likely results. Some parrots, in their confusion,

Your parrot must learn to accept that you are his 'flock leader'.

will also take to plucking out their feathers. The solution is for the human keeper to give firm boundaries and guidance for behaviour.

BE CONSISTENT

Many parrot keepers make the mistake of giving in to their parrot's demands through misguided kindness. It is thoroughly confusing to a bird if commands are half-hearted or inconsistent. If you relent when your parrot nips you, he will only bite harder the next time – parrots learn quickly and never forget.

TRAINING METHODS

You should train your parrot using positive methods, encouraging every desired behaviour with words of praise. Remember that, because parrots watch our facial expressions closely, you should smile and look positive throughout each training session.

Bad behaviour should be ignored, not punished. The aim is to teach your parrot to obey you because of the praise and responses he receives in return. If unwanted behaviour is ignored, your bird will have no reason to repeat it.

Training is best done in a room with few distractions, such as a spare bedroom or the bathroom. Never become angry with your pet for not understanding or obeying you. What is simple and obvious to you is a whole new world for your bird. Hitting a bird is cruel and will destroy the trust your parrot has in you. If the training session is not going well, simply stop, and try again another time. Your bird may be tired or out of sorts. We all need our quiet times when we want to be left alone and parrots are no exception.

TRAINING EXERCISES

Start regular training sessions once your parrot has begun responding to you and is likely to enjoy the interaction. If you have more than one bird, train them separately.

A couple of sessions a day is enough. Wait for a time during the day when the bird is attentive, then keep the lesson to just a few minutes. Do not wait until your parrot has got bored or irritated before stopping. By keeping training times short and making them fun, they will be regarded by the bird as something enjoyable and quicker progress will be made as a result. Always use a release word, such as "Finished", at the end of each training session.

STEP UP

Getting a parrot to step on to your hand is the first important lesson. With a larger, or potentially aggressive, parrot, you may prefer to start training using a wooden perch. Otherwise, once the parrot is at ease with having your hand close to him in the cage, get him to step on to it by saying "Up" and holding your hand against the bird's lower chest, just above his feet. With gentle pressure, the bird will tip slightly backwards and will naturally step up to right himself. Repeat the exercise until your

◄ *Progress in small stages. To begin with, this Cockatiel is getting used to the presence of a hand in his cage.*

► *Now this Black-Headed Caique is confident enough to step on to a hand.*

◄ *Out in the open, he can be taught to step up again, or on to the hand of another family member.*

parrot automatically steps up on to your hand or arm every time you ask.

STEP DOWN

To train your bird to step down, hold your hand just below the perch and say "Down", perhaps encouraging him with a food treat held in the other hand. Parrots prefer to step up rather than down, so this skill may take a little longer to accomplish. Repeat both commands often, until they become second nature to your pet. Always stick to the single-word commands like "Up" and "Down", rather than any complicated phrase or sentence, and do not vary or add to them.

CONFIDENT HANDLING

When your bird is stepping up or down on to your hand for the first time, he may investigate the unfamiliar 'perch' with his beak. He is not trying to bite you, so do not panic and pull away. Instead, instil your parrot with confidence, by keeping your hand firm and steady and lavishing your pet with plenty of praise.

If your parrot is still nervous of your hand, he may nip you deliberately. Difficult though it is, try not to over-react by jumping

or shouting, or you will make the situation worse – once your pet knows he can achieve a reaction by biting you, he will do it again!

STEPPING OUT

Once your parrot is confidently stepping on and off your hand, you will want to remove him from the cage for his period of free time. Before attempting this, make sure all windows and doors are shut, and inform other family members that the bird is free.

Some birds are reluctant to leave the safety of their cage and may back off or hang on to the sides as you try to lift them out. However, correct training means that it is you, rather than your parrot, who decides what is going to happen, so do not just leave the cage door open for your bird to fly out when he feels like it. This will give him the message that he, rather than you, is in charge. Instead, persevere, encouraging your bird with praise or small treats, until he will stay on your hand long enough to be lifted out. Once relaxed with you, your parrot should be encouraged to step on to the hands of other family members.

STAYING IN

US parrot psychologist Liz Wilson

Stroke your parrot gently so that he learns to enjoy being handled.

has good advice if your parrot is too nervous to come near you, let alone step on to your hand, allowing himself to be lifted out. The following procedure can also be applied if your parrot becomes over-possessive about his cage, displaying aggression when you come near.

- Remove dishes, toys and the base tray from the cage.
- Take the cage to another room. A small room, such as the bathroom, is ideal, as you will then be in close proximity to your bird.
- Slowly and gently, tip the cage upside down and your bird will venture out. Remove the cage from the room.
- Settle down with a book or magazine and be prepared for a long wait. Pay no attention to the bird if he approaches you, but just carry on reading. Away from his cage and familiar surroundings, your parrot will be looking to you for reassurance (as you will be the one recognisable thing in the room).
- Go at the bird's pace, speaking to him gently and making no sudden moves.
- You may need to repeat this procedure a few times, but, with time and patience, your bird will lose his fear and look on you as a trusted ally, rather than the enemy.
- If your parrot is otherwise tame, but still reluctant to leave his cage, offer special food treats or toys once he is out, so that the environment outside the cage becomes a more inviting place to be.

"NO!"

This is an essential basic command for parrots. Use the word firmly whenever the bird is doing something unacceptable, and sound as if you mean it. When commanding "No!", accompany it with a very stern, accusing look and your bird will quickly get the message.

TOILET-TRAINING

Teaching your parrot to go to the toilet at a place convenient to you is not difficult and certainly saves on housework and washing! As you become familiar with your pet's body language, you will recognise when he is about to defecate. When a dropping looks imminent, quickly lift the bird (gently holding his tail upwards) to the designated 'toilet'. This could be your parrot's playstand or any other suitable perch placed over newspaper. Give a set command, e.g. "Action!". Praise each success, and your bird will soon get the idea.

DEVELOPING RELATIONSHIPS

Once your parrot is obeying the above commands – without question and every time – now is the time to try to build on the trust between you and your parrot and develop a more affectionate bond.

TRUST AND TOUCH

Many parrots are wary of being touched, although few can resist a tickle at the back of the neck through the cage bars. Touch is an important part of the relationship between parrot and keeper and can be introduced gradually, once your bird will step on your hand and you can lift him out of his cage.

The inquisitive parrot wants to be involved with everything that is going on.

Let your pet sit with you on the sofa as you watch television. In time, he will enjoy a stroke and cuddle, or snuggling into a shirt or jumper. As always, never rush the process. As your parrot becomes tamer and more confident, he will welcome physical affection more.

PARROTS AND SHOULDERS

Although many parrot keepers do it, allowing even a tame parrot on to your shoulder is not a good idea. That powerful beak could inflict serious damage to your face – it may even take out an eye – and it is just not worth the risk. Parrots can quickly become tangled up in long hair or jewellery and start to panic, which will certainly make you panic, too!

If your bird has already got into the habit of sitting on your shoulder, it may take a while to retrain him to stay on your hand or arm, but persevere until he has learnt that shoulders are out of bounds.

Another important point to remember is that, by keeping your pet below eye level, you are reinforcing the message that he is below you in the pecking order. A parrot perched on your hand or arm, at or below chest level, will be far more compliant.

COPING WITH STRANGERS

Even a well-socialised parrot, that loves to snuggle into your jumper, can become hostile if approached by a stranger. As with humans, parrots do not like everyone they meet and this should be respected. Your bird may not like visitors because he is frightened by them. If this is the case, keep visitors at a distance from the cage until your parrot has become used to them.

A point worth bearing in mind is that, at some point, you will need to leave your parrot with someone else – when you go on holiday for example, or perhaps into hospital. If your parrot has become used to attention and handling from trusted humans other than his keeper, he will be far less likely to become stressed if you have to leave him for a week or two. There have been cases where a previously unplucked parrot has pulled out all his feathers when his keeper has gone away on holiday. Avoid this by letting your parrot mix with as many people as possible.

6 *Having Fun*

Your bird can be considered truly tame and trusting when he lies back in your hand, with his feet in the air, and lets you tickle his stomach. In the wild, a bird would never adopt this position because of the threat from predators. Once your parrot has reached this stage, he is ready to learn tricks and to have fun. Learning to talk, however, can start much sooner, even if the bird is not fully tame.

LEARNING TO TALK

Many species, such as the Yellow-Headed Amazon and, most notably, the African Grey, will learn to mimic words, tunes and household sounds, without any effort on the part of the keeper. Some species will not progress beyond a few words and whistles, which they continually repeat, while others choose to stick to their natural parrot calls.

Even with species that usually mimic well, there will be some individuals who prefer not to bother. This often happens where more than one bird is kept. Two or more birds will communicate with each other in their own language, and may not feel the need to use human speech to interact with their keeper.

INFORMAL TRAINING

Parrots start talking at different ages, so do not be disappointed if your young bird does not start chatting as soon as you bring him home. Parrots tend to respond most readily to the higher-pitched voices of women and children, particularly when the inflection is varied and exaggerated.

The important thing is to chat to your bird all the time – as you come in or go out, when putting fresh food and water into the cage, and as you pass him on his playstand. He will be listening all the time and will want to respond.

Hand-reared babies usually start talking quite early on as they have grown up hearing human speech around them.

In time, you will start to hear a change in the usual parrot chatter, prior to recognisable words emerging. If you want your bird to learn a particular word or phrase, repeat it often, at appropriate times during the day, so that it becomes associated with a particular action in the bird's mind. For example, say "Hi there" as you come into the room, "See you later" as you go out of the door, and "Dinner time" as you put food in the dish. Use a bright tone of voice to get your pet's attention.

Hawk Head Parrot: Choose a time of day when your parrot is at his most responsive.

TRAINING SESSIONS

More intensive teaching can be given with regular training sessions. Choose a time of day when your parrot is most responsive and the house is quiet. Conduct the speech-training in a different room from the one your parrot usually lives in. Keep the lessons to just a few minutes each time.

Repeat the word or phrase you want to teach, using a lively, interesting voice and saying it in the same way every time. If teaching a phrase or sentence, teach one part at a time, before moving on to the next and finally getting the bird to put the whole thing together. Stop the lesson when you feel you no longer have your bird's attention. Repeat the same words at other times during the day and, sooner or later, you will have success.

An alternative teaching method is to place the bird in an empty cage and to cover the cage with a cloth for five to ten minutes. During this period, repeat the words you want the bird to learn. With nothing to distract him, and only the sound of your voice to focus on, parrots can learn quickly this way. After this brief training session, the bird can be returned to his usual cage or playstand. However, most parrots learn to mimic without intensive training of this kind.

PRACTICE

When your parrot first starts to mimic speech, the words may not be distinguishable from all his other parrot chatter. Over time this will improve. You may want to record the lessons on to a tape, to be played when you are not around. Alternatively, there are commercial speech tapes and CDs available, although there is no substitute for personal contact between you and your pet.

USEFUL APPLICATIONS

Training your parrot to talk can be more than entertainment. If a parrot becomes lost or stolen,

his ability to recite his name and home telephone number increases the chance of reuniting him with his keeper.

WORD OF WARNING

Once your bird starts talking, you may find he never stops. Think very carefully about the words you teach your pet, as you may be listening to them repeated all day long! Be mindful of the language you use around your parrot, as, once he has taken to mimicry, your pet will repeat everything he hears, including swear words!

TRICK-TRAINING

Parrots have a need for self-expression, so experiment with simple games your bird shows an aptitude for. A parrot that has never learnt to play may need to be shown how much fun can be had!

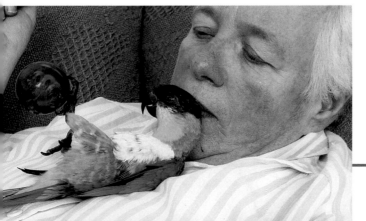

Teaching tricks provides mental stimulation as well as giving you the opportunity to interact with your parrot.

African Greys are quick to learn, and will love mastering new tricks.

WHY?

Teaching a parrot to do tricks is a great way of providing mental stimulation. Macaws and Cockatoos are known for their ability to learn quite involved tricks, such as cycling along a tightrope, although much can also be achieved with Greys, Amazons and others.

WHEN?

Many birds will enjoy sharing a shower with their keeper in the morning, or being included in daily activities – helping with the dusting, or writing a shopping list, for example. If your parrot enjoys this, you should have no difficulty in teaching him specific party pieces.

WHAT?

Have fun with a small mirror; find a basket, paper sack or cardboard box, and play hide-and-seek (parrots love hiding); roll and chase a ball together; hide a peanut in your hand, and let your bird prise it out; basically, do whatever activity your pet particularly enjoys. Some keepers teach their bird to take a nut or seed from their own mouth, but this is not advisable for health reasons.

Parrot toy outlets supply miniature basketball sets, bird-size roller skates, scooters and skateboards. Teaching a bird to skate or ride a bike will take time, but it is achievable. Your biggest obstacle would be your pet's fear of something unfamiliar. If so, let him see you playing with the new item first and then introduce him to it very slowly and carefully.

Of course, there is no need to spend money on expensive trick-training equipment. Just one example is to teach your bird to pick up small coins and drop them into a pot.

HOW?

Once your bird is fully tame, start with simple tricks that use his existing natural skills – picking up small items, flying, turning

The trick does not need to be complex to be fun – this Cockatiel is naturally curious, so it is easy to make 'piano playing' part of his repertoire.

somersaults, etc. Build on actions he already enjoys doing. By doing the training in a small room with few distractions – the bathroom again – your parrot is more likely to concentrate on what you are teaching him. As with all training, keep the lessons short and fun. Be patient, and give your parrot every reason to want to do the trick – maybe a small food treat, or a tickle on the back of his neck, every time he performs even partly successfully.

Break down each trick into simple stages, teaching each one in sequence. Keep things simple and use the same word of praise each time, for instance "Good!". Always end on a high note, when things are going well. If things do not, simply try again and, of course, never use any form of punishment.

HOW LONG?

Ten or fifteen minutes is long enough for any trick-training session, although it can be repeated later in the day. Stop before your pet starts to get bored. Aim to end when the bird has just carried out a successful move, say the praise word and finish there.

This trick provides plenty of occupation, and most parrots will keep going until all the money has been 'counted', particularly if a reward is on offer.

AN EXAMPLE

If your parrot enjoys playing with toys, you might want to teach him to play ball.

The trick could be broken down in the following way, with each successful move being rewarded with a treat or the praise word.

- Your parrot picks up a small, soft ball
- He picks up the ball and throws it
- You throw the ball back and the parrot returns it to you.

Any trick you want to teach can be achieved in this way, the bird learning each stage independently, and then putting them together.

7 *Problem Behaviours*

When a pet parrot shows disturbed behaviour, such as screaming, biting or feather-plucking, one of the following reasons normally applies:

- Not knowing his place within the household
- Over-indulgence when a baby
- Lack of consistent discipline and training
- Insecurity caused by repeated re-homing
- Long periods left alone in his cage
- Insufficient mental stimulation
- Attention-seeking
- Adolescence
- Seasonal breeding condition.

Some of the more common problem behaviours are dealt with in this chapter. More serious ones may require the help of an avian behaviourist. He or she will observe how you interact with your parrot and should be able to offer good advice on how to change the situation for the better.

ADOLESCENCE

During adolescence and the advent of hormones, even a previously loving and well-cared-for bird may surprise his keeper by suddenly taking to screaming or nipping. This period has been

It is essential that the adolescent parrot knows who is boss.

described as the 'terrible twos' and is a common reason for a parrot being passed from home to home.

This temporary, unsettled state will eventually pass, provided your parrot has already been taught the rules for acceptable behaviour and is otherwise under control. Teenage tantrums can be kept at manageable levels if the bird has never been allowed to believe he is the boss. You can also modify his diet to improve his behaviour (see page 73). Eventually, your parrot should revert to his affectionate and docile self.

CONTROL MEASURES

Some parrot keepers choose to have their bird's wings clipped during adolescence. Clipping is a common solution for aggressive behaviour caused by hormones.

The debate over the necessity or cruelty of wing-clipping is still ongoing (see page 72). Whatever your views, you may need to consider a temporary wing-clip if the bird you are trying to train is proving too aggressive to bring under control. In these cases, curbing the bird's ability to hurtle round the room whenever he feels like it may be the best solution.

Wing-clipping should always be carried out by an experienced professional (see page 72).

Even if you do not like the idea of wing-clipping, remember that, given time, the feathers will grow out again. In the meantime, your parrot should prove more amenable, easier to interact with, and training can be got under way. Curbing flight is also a solution in cases of bullying in the aviary, for instance when a male is harassing a female.

BREEDING CONDITION

Aggression towards the keeper is also common when a mature bird

A parrot may become aggressive with the onset of sexual maturity.

It is important to avoid the dangers of a parrot bonding too closely with one person.

comes into breeding condition – usually in the spring. Sexual maturity begins at three to four years of age in the larger species, and slightly younger in smaller parrots.

The signs of this condition are behavioural rather than physical, and include behaviour such as aggression, sexual behaviour towards humans, nest-making, and egg-laying.

OVER-BONDING

Problematic breeding-related behaviour often arises when a parrot has bonded too closely with one member of the family. A bonded pet parrot will regard his keeper as his mate, which can present problems during the breeding season. For example, your bird may try to feed you his own regurgitated dinner to prove his devotion!

Over-bonding is much easier to prevent than it is to cure. Involving your whole family with your parrot, so that he does not fixate on you, will help prevent over-bonding from arising.

If over-bonding has become a problem, teach your bird to step off your hand on to a family member's. Repeat until your pet has become used to handling by other people. Wait until the breeding season has passed, however. Your parrot may be more inclined to nip during this time, so play safe and don't let anyone handle the bird while the potentially aggressive behaviour lasts.

Once your parrot has come out of breeding condition, practise making him go to other family members until he will do so without aggression. Always ensure that you supervise this process carefully, however, especially where children are involved. Likewise, only allow trusted, careful people to handle your bird, as injury can easily be inflicted by either party.

If your parrot is directing his courtship towards you, trying to mate with your hand or arm, distract him by removing him to his playstand with a new, interesting item to investigate. If the parrot continues to try to mate with his toys (or you), and it is becoming problematic, your vet may recommend hormonal treatment.

EGG-LAYING
A female in breeding condition may repeatedly lay eggs or try to build a nest from torn-up newspaper at the bottom of the cage. If this happens, do not remove the eggs. Your parrot may try to lay more, becoming seriously weakened as a result. Some birds, Greys in particular, will often scratch about at the bottom of their cage and hide under the newspaper. This is normal behaviour, however, and should not be confused with nest-making.

MATING
When breeding behaviour is proving problematic, some keepers decide that their pet would be happier with a mate, living in an aviary, with the opportunity to breed. This is certainly the best solution in some cases, but not all. Think carefully before making this big change in your pet's life. If he has always lived in the sitting room and is used to having human companionship, being moved to an outdoor aviary (or an indoor bird room) may be too stressful for him. You will also need to ensure that your bird will get on well with his new partner.

If you have decided to let your parrot breed, and are moving him to an outdoor aviary, make the change gradually. Your parrot will need time to become accustomed to his new home and the corresponding change of temperature. Introduce the new mate with great care, keeping the birds caged separately for a few days while you watch their reaction to each other.

Only when you are sure they are friendly should you put them together. Even then, continue to watch closely for any signs of

Finding a mate can sometimes help to solve behavioural problems.

bullying. This is particularly important in the case of Cockatoos, when the male bird may become extremely aggressive towards the female.

One final point to watch out for is that, once your parrot has bonded with his new mate, he is unlikely to show the same affection towards you.

SCREAMING

All parrots make a fair amount of noise from time to time. If you keep a Macaw or a Cockatoo, for example, you will certainly need tolerant neighbours. Eclectus, Pionus, Senegals and Cockatiels are some of the quieter species. Regular calling at dawn and dusk, and alarm cries, are natural for parrots, as is the ear-piercing screeching they sometimes indulge in just because they feel like it! Fortunately, there is much the keeper can do to keep noise levels within reasonable limits.

By maintaining a quiet environment, and speaking or singing to your parrot in a soft voice, he is less likely to develop into a raucous bird. In homes where the television or stereo is always on, and people are talking loudly above the sound, the pet parrot will be stimulated into competing with the noise around him.

Parrots copy each other, and a normally peaceable individual may well imitate the scream of a noisier friend. If you are thinking of acquiring a new bird, bear this in mind. Other reasons for screaming include hunger or thirst, breeding condition, illness, fatigue, over-stimulation, boredom and attention-seeking.

COPING WITH SCREAMING

Your parrot's screaming may be his only way of letting you know something is wrong. He may want a change of food, or be unhappy with the position of his cage or the surrounding environment. If your parrot starts screaming for no apparent reason, take a long look at his housing conditions and routine, and see if something needs changing.

However, if you come running every time your parrot screams, you are giving him every reason to scream more often and more loudly. Your parrot wants your company and attention and he gets it when you react in this way. Do not scream back to keep him quiet – your bird will love this and will simply try to outdo you! Instead, leave the room when the

Screaming may be the result of boredom, so try providing some mental stimulation for your parrot.

screaming starts and only come back in once the bird is quiet. This is the time to take him out of his cage (unless he is in an aggressive mood, in which case leave him where he is) and lavish him with praise and attention. He should soon learn that he gets attention only when he is quiet.

BITING

This unpleasant habit can lead to real problems in the relationship between parrot and keeper. The situation becomes worse as the parrot tries to take control by biting more often, and the keeper becomes fearful and less willing to handle the bird.

Certain species are likely to be more aggressive than others. Male Cockatoos, in particular, can be highly dangerous during the breeding season and, at the other end of the size scale, even the little Lovebird can become nippy as he matures.

CAUSES

Aggressive biting is not normal behaviour for a parrot. A wild-caught parrot, or one that has been previously mistreated, may bite from fear. Captive-bred birds tend to bite when they have over-bonded with their keeper, and are jealous of the keeper's human partner; if they have been subjected to little training and discipline; if they are going through the 'terrible twos'; or if they are in breeding condition. A parrot that has been allowed to perch above eye-level will believe he is superior to his keeper, and this can also lead to biting as he attempts to maintain control.

A tendency to bite normally begins quite innocently, when the baby bird starts trying things out with his beak. One day he squeezes a bit too hard on your finger and gets a noisy reaction as you jump up and squeal. This is regarded as great fun by the baby, who nips harder the next time just to see what happens.

There are no excuses for biting, but there are occasions when it is more understandable. For example, if your parrot is unwell, he may display uncharacteristic behaviour. If you suspect this, do not delay in consulting an avian vet. Similarly, all parrots need some time on their own, which should be respected. Your bird's body language will tell you when he does not want to be petted – ignore it at your peril!

STOPPING BITING

Again, as with most behavioural problems, prevention is better than a cure. If your parrot tries to bite you, you need to teach him, immediately, that nipping and biting are unacceptable. Never hit a bird for biting. Instead, gently remove your pet's beak, look him in the eye, say, "No!" in a stern voice, and then return your pet to his cage. Ignore him for a short while. Parrots hate being ignored and will soon learn that biting is non-profitable.

The important thing is to show no fear yourself. This can be difficult if you have already been

If you remain calm, your parrot will sense that you are in charge, and this should help to overcome his insecurity.

bitten! However, your parrot will be taking the lead from your attitude. If he senses that you are fully in charge of the situation, this will resolve his own insecurity.

Sometimes, despite your best efforts, you will not be able to trust your bird not to bite. If this is the case, let him sit with you on the sofa when you are relaxing in the evening, but do not make any move towards him. Ignore your parrot and carry on with what you are doing. Hold a food treat and let the bird nibble on this until he is stepping on to your hand without fear. Continue to ignore him completely as he does this. In

this way, your pet will cease to see you, or your hand, as a threat.

FEATHER-PLUCKING

Feather-plucked parrots are not seen in the wild, so it follows that the condition is brought about by certain aspects of captivity. African Greys and Cockatoos, as well as some Macaws, seem particularly prone to it.

Feather-plucking can range in seriousness from simply chewing at a few feathers, through to serious self-mutilation, where the flesh itself is damaged and the feathers can never grow back.

CAUSES

Once birds start to pull out their feathers, it can become an addiction that is very hard to stop. In some cases, the bird's normal moult leads to over-enthusiastic preening, which then becomes a habit.

Where more than one bird is kept, the culprit may be another parrot. This becomes obvious when feathers go missing from the head. The cause may be over-crowding if the birds are kept in an aviary, or aggression from a mate.

If your bird starts plucking out his feathers, first rule out any possible medical causes. Your vet can check for conditions such as allergies, parasites, liver disease, lead or zinc poisoning (from some cage wire) and infections. If your bird is eating mainly seed, and refusing fresh fruit and vegetables, this is also a possible cause. Your vet will be able to advise on changing the diet and adding vitamin supplements.

By far the most common reasons for feather-plucking are:

- Long periods left alone in the cage.
- Lack of human company and attention.
- Lack of mental stimulation.
- No opportunity to bathe.
- Insufficient sleep.
- Change of environment (even a new toy in the cage).
- Injury or bad wing-clipping.
- The need for a mate.
- Insecurity due to lack of discipline and training from the keeper.

SOLUTIONS

Give careful consideration to your parrot's environment and routine, and make whatever changes are needed. Do all you can, but do not lose heart – even the most experienced, devoted parrot keepers will sometimes have a bird who, despite all their best efforts, continues to pluck from time to time. In severe cases, an Elizabethan collar may be fitted by your vet to try to curb the habit and to allow time for healing.

A bored and lonely bird will often resort to feather-plucking.

DESTRUCTION

Parrots love to chew! With a plentiful supply of natural branches and wooden toys, the beak will be kept in trim, and the destructive chewing of furniture through boredom should not pose too big a problem. However, some of the bigger parrots can quickly destroy a coffee table or skirting board if left unsupervised for any length of time. This is one instance where your bird needs to have learnt the meaning of "No!" (see page 50).

SPECIAL CASES

Two popular parrot species are worth a special mention as, without careful training, they can be particularly prone to behavioural problems when they reach maturity.

All parrots are very intelligent and none more so than the sensitive Grey and affectionate Cockatoo. Careful hand-rearing and weaning by the breeder, together with early lessons in acceptable behaviour, are important for these birds. If the new keeper continues with the social training, establishes a consistent routine, and provides his bird with plenty of attention and occupation, potential problems will be avoided.

Many African Greys and Cockatoos are passed from home to home through no fault of their own. Insufficient socialisation has resulted in their being branded 'nasty birds', because they panic and bite when a hand comes into the cage. Fear is expressed by characteristic growling from a Grey, or hissing from a Cockatoo. However, even long-standing problem behaviours can be righted with commitment and patience from the keeper.

AFRICAN GREYS

African Greys need plenty of freedom from their cages, toys to play with, and branches to chew on. A secure, well-occupied Grey is far less likely to pull out his feathers than a bird left in an empty cage all day. Remember, too, that Greys are easily frightened. Unfamiliar objects, noises or lights, may scare your bird badly, so introduce anything new with great care.

COCKATOOS

However tempting, do not over-indulge your cuddly baby Cockatoo. These birds bond particularly closely with their keepers and will become confused when the novelty wears off and

Unfortunately, African Greys may be passed from home to home, through no fault of their own.

they suddenly find themselves confined to their cage.

Teach your bird, from the start, that he cannot be with you at all times. Let him become accustomed to playing on his own in the cage for certain periods of the day, while you are out of the room. If this has always been part of a regular routine, your Cockatoo will have no problem with it. The alternative is a bird that screams every time you are out of sight – distressing for both the bird and you, and easily avoidable.

If you take on a Cockatoo, be prepared to give up a good deal of your time and attention to this most demanding pet. Keep him happy and stimulated with plenty of toys and wooden items to chew, cardboard boxes to play in, and games he can share with you. The result will be a delightful and loving parrot, and a well-integrated member of the family.

8 Grooming And Health

Maintaining a simple but thorough care plan will help to ensure that your parrot leads a long and happy life.

GROOMING
To keep your parrot in top condition, you will need to ensure that he has plenty of opportunity to exercise and to groom himself. You will, in addition, have to perform some grooming functions yourself.

BATH-TIME
Some parrots love splashing about in a shallow bath of water, while others hate the idea. If you keep one of the latter variety, gently introduce your bird to water by misting him regularly by means of a plant sprayer. Test the temperature first to ensure the water is pleasantly warm. It will feel quite cool once sprayed into the air, and your already reluctant

Misting the feathers with a plant sprayer is an essential aid to feather condition.

bird may object. Allow plenty of time for the feathers to become completely dry before your bird is returned to his cage for the night.

NAILS
With plenty of rough-wood perching in your parrot's cage, your pet's nails and beak should stay naturally trimmed. However,

Opposite: Blue and Gold Macaw.

71

if they become overgrown, perhaps because your parrot is elderly and less energetic, they may need to be manually trimmed. If so, always take your parrot to the vet for the first clipping. Your vet will be able to demonstrate how to perform the procedure safely.

If you clip your parrot's nails, it is important that you do not put your pet under stress. Many keepers wrap their birds in a towel, to restrain them during clipping, but your parrot will hate this confinement. Keep grooming times to just a few minutes. Work quickly and confidently, talking gently to your bird to help keep him relaxed.

When wing-clipping is considered necessary, both wings should be clipped evenly.

WING-CLIPPING

Wing-clipping is a very controversial procedure in the parrot-keeping community. There is certainly a strong case for allowing a bird his natural ability and desire to fly. However, it should be balanced against the danger of keeping a fully-flighted bird in the home, where a door or window might be left open, or where there are hot cooker tops and other potential hazards. Most experts now agree that all baby birds should be allowed to develop their muscles and flying skills fully before wings are clipped.

Sometimes, wing-clipping can prevent an injured parrot from harming himself further, or can calm an aggressive bird so that taming and training can take place.

It should be remembered that, as long as wing-clipping is carried out by an experienced and competent professional, flight feathers will always grow back. That professional should be a veterinary surgeon who specialises in birds, or a parrot keeper experienced in the correct procedure.

When the procedure is undertaken, both wings should be evenly and carefully clipped, just enough to slow the bird down temporarily, but without robbing him of flight altogether. Serious injury can result from falls caused by the clipping of one wing only, which unbalances the bird. Over-severe clipping can also lead to injury from falls, as well as problems with feather regrowth and the inevitable stress to the bird.

With E.B. Cravens' *Progressive Wing Clip* method, the flight feathers are carefully clipped in progressive stages. The bird's ability to go too far or too fast is gradually reduced in this way, while still leaving him able to manoeuvre and to land safely.

HEALTHY EATING
You will know yourself how a few days of healthy eating can make a big difference to how you feel. It will come as no surprise, then, that what you give your parrot to eat will have a direct bearing on his mood and behaviour.

GOOD EATING HABITS
In the past, it was accepted practice to provide a parrot with no more than a daily bowl of seed and a cuttlefish bone. There was a general lack of knowledge about a parrot's dietary needs, and the depressed-looking caged bird, with his feathers dull and tatty, was a common sight.

The good news is that, with all the recent research into parrot diets and the many excellent pelleted foods on the market today, it has never been easier to ensure that your bird stays in top condition.

KEEP IT NATURAL
Research the diet that your particular species of parrot would be eating in the wild, and aim to provide him with similar foodstuffs. All parrots will eat a

Protein is derived from eating nuts.

wide variety of foods when foraging for themselves, with raw fruits and green foods making up a high percentage of their intake. Protein is obtained from nuts and seeds, and, occasionally, insects. Remember, though, that a wild bird flies in search of food, using up energy and calories as it does so. Nuts and seeds are high in fat and these should be given sparingly to the less active parrot, who may otherwise become obese.

COMPLETE FOODS

A species-specific pelleted or extruded diet can form a good basis for your bird's daily nutritional requirements, provided that a variety of fresh fruit and vegetables is also eaten each day. The pure, organic pelleted feeds now available are dull in appearance compared with the other brightly coloured commercial foods. However, they have the benefit of containing only natural ingredients, and, interestingly, have been found to curb feather-plucking in some cases.

SEASONAL FOODS

A free source of seasonal green foods and berries can be found in fields and hedgerows. Avoid

A species-specific extruded diet provides for basic nutritional needs.

gathering foods from roadsides, and always make sure that you wash the produce carefully before giving it to your birds. If you have any doubts about whether it is safe to give your parrot any particular type of food, then do not give it. Rowan, hawthorn, honeysuckle, pyracantha, elderberries, rosehips, blackberries, chickweed, dandelion, milk thistle and seeding grasses are all safe foods that your parrot will enjoy.

FRUIT AND VEGETABLES

Your parrot will also enjoy some household fruit and vegetables.

Some species (e.g. Amazons, Cockatoos and Macaws), like to nibble at a piece of apple or carrot held in their foot. Your parrot will also probably appreciate some intricate foods that take time to eat, such as halved walnuts, peanuts in their shells, or half a pomegranate.

FOODS TO AVOID

There are certain foods that should always be avoided. Chocolate and avocado are considered poisonous to parrots and, in some cases, have proved fatal. Salty, fatty foods, such as potato crisps and salted peanuts, should never be fed. A more surprising food to be

A plain biscuit is fine for an occasional treat.

avoided is lettuce, which should never be given in large amounts. However, your pet will enjoy sharing food treats with you, so give a piece of plain biscuit, monkey nuts in the shell, or a small piece of cheese, which make much healthier options.

It may be necessary to avoid certain foods at particular times. For example, aggressive behaviour, occurring when a pet parrot comes into breeding condition, can be lessened by cutting down on protein. Reducing foods such as nuts, seeds, chicken bones, peas and beans, will all help to improve your parrot's temper.

SUNFLOWER SEEDS

A diet high in sunflower seeds is a nutritional disaster. It provides far too much fat and lacks the essential vitamins and minerals needed for good health. Unfortunately, we often hear of sunflower seed 'junkies' – literally, parrots addicted to this food, to the exclusion of anything else. Apart from the serious health problems that can result, such as lack of calcium and vitamins A and D, sunflower-seed diets can lead to chronic feather-plucking. Always keep sunflower seeds to a minimum.

Some parrots may be reluctant to try new types of food.

IMPROVING YOUR PET'S DIET

If your parrot has only ever been fed sunflower seeds, with the occasional chip or chicken bone from the dinner table, you may find it very difficult to introduce healthier foods, such as fresh fruit and vegetables. However, it is vital for your bird's health and balanced behaviour that bad eating habits are broken and replaced with more suitable foods. This process can take a long time, as new foods need to be introduced slowly. A new bunch of fresh broccoli may be welcomed by an Amazon or a Macaw, but may be regarded with fear by a nervous African Grey.

Do not be tempted to give in if your parrot steadfastly turns up his beak at anything new. Instead, be patient and prepared for the long haul. Add tiny pieces of grape, sweetcorn and grated carrot, for example, to the bird's usual food. Keep it colourful, and, if you think you might achieve better results, try giving cooked vegetables rather than raw. Most of the new foods will probably be thrown out, but, in trying to get to the seed, some fruit and vegetables will inadvertently be eaten.

PARROT PSYCHOLOGY

As with a human child that steadfastly refuses to eat his greens, you may find it necessary to use some psychology to persuade your parrot to eat more healthily.

A good trick is to limit feeds to twice a day to stimulate the bird's enthusiasm. Never leave your parrot for long periods without food. Depending on the species, parrots will eat up to twice their own body weight in one day, the food being quickly digested and eliminated.

Also try eating some of the new foods in front of your parrot, letting him see how delicious the fruit or vegetable is and how much you are enjoying it. Don't offer the food to your bird until he has become really interested, though, or he will become wise to the trick.

Some parrots will take readily to new foods, while others will remain suspicious for months. However, most come round eventually, and the health and behavioural payoffs are well worth it.

REFUSAL TO EAT

It is most important that you make sure your parrot is not starving while you try to convert him to a healthier diet. Cockatoos, in particular, can be stubborn about trying anything new. If you suspect your pet is not eating enough, reduce the quantities of the new food or stop giving it altogether, and revert to the old diet for a while before trying again. In these cases, vitamin and mineral supplements will be needed in the interim period. Do not accept them as a substitute, however. The final aim is to replace completely the old diet with the healthy new one.

FEEDING PRACTICES

Food is an important part of your parrot's day, so make it fun and watch your bird thrive as a result. If we 'think parrot', we can see that the same food each day is going to be very boring indeed. By feeding our birds in this monotonous way, we are providing none of the activity and stimulation they would be getting when feeding in a natural environment.

MAKE FOOD FUN

- Vary the colour, texture and smell of the food you give.
- Hang bunches of greens, seeding grasses, or edible flowers in bud (e.g. daisies,

Introduce variety into the diet, and try to make feeding times fun.

marigolds or nasturtiums) from the cage top or playstand.
- Give fruits and vegetables that need ingenuity to open and eat, such as peas in the pod or mandarins.
- Hide small food treats for your bird to search out – he will soon catch on and enjoy the challenge.

DINNER COMPANIONS

In the wild, parrots eat communally. In captivity, parrots love to join in family meals. You may like to share your lunch-time salad with your parrot, giving him small sticks of celery and carrot to nibble on. However, do not be tempted to indulge your pet with unsuitable human 'junk' foods.

VARIETY

Just like humans, birds can tire of a particular food for a while, even if it was a favourite before, so be prepared to change the items offered. A chicken bone with a little meat left on, or a piece of toast, will provide an enjoyable variation to the diet. Wherever possible, stick to organic foods.

HEALTH AND HYGIENE

Buy dry parrot food from a reliable outlet with a quick turnover, to ensure freshness. Also make sure fresh foods are carefully washed. Parrots can be surprisingly sensitive to bacteria on foods. You will need to clean the food and water dishes on a daily basis, to prevent the build-up of any harmful bacteria.

HEALTH CARE
By knowing your parrot, and watching for any change in his behaviour, you will quickly know if he is unwell.

CHOOSING A VET
It is a good idea to choose your vet before you buy your parrot, so that you are prepared for any eventuality immediately.

It is vital that you choose an experienced avian vet. Vets specialising in birds are few and far between.

However, as birds have very particular needs, and expert advice should always be sought, be prepared to travel some distance.

HEALTH CHECKS
Keep an eye on your parrot for any sign of ill health. Each parrot has his own unique personality, but most are active and vocal, making their presence felt throughout the day.

A bird that never moves far from his perch and utters few sounds may, therefore, be unwell or under-nourished rather than just 'well behaved'. If in any doubt, consult your vet immediately.

Natural instinct makes a bird hide any illness for as long as possible and the 'wait and see' approach might mean you leave it too late for anything to be done.

Symptoms of ill health include:
- A sleepy, fluffed-up appearance.
- Inability to perch.
- Messy vent (the area under the tail).
- Discharge from nostrils, or laboured breathing.
- Coughing.
- Constantly nibbling at feathers.

Observe your parrot closely, so you will spot any signs of ill health at an early stage.

Your parrot deserves special understanding.

CARING FOR THE SICK PARROT

If your parrot becomes injured or unwell, always consult your vet. Keep your pet warm and quiet until treatment can be given. Make sure that he has easy access to food and water, and remember that he may not have the ability to easily take either. There are some excellent first-aid nutrient formulas now available, and it is a good idea to have a supply to hand for emergencies when your pet has stopped eating.

HOLISTIC APPROACH

Colour may play an important part in the health and wellbeing of a bird. Holistic parrot therapist Dr Rosina Sonnenschmidt describes green, blue and gold (the colours of the trees and sky) as the life colours of birds, and suggests introducing them into the captive parrot's environment.

Homoeopathic and herbal remedies have been used successfully by parrot keepers for many conditions, both physical and psychological. These complementary remedies often work well in conjunction with orthodox medicine, but you should always consult your avian vet before introducing any complementary therapies. Parrots deserve understanding and care. Good luck with your bird.